A Little Book
about
God's Great Love

Written by Carol Sullivan Johnson on behalf of The Barn Church Fellowship.

All inquiries are welcome to: contact.the.barnchurch@gmail.com

This booklet may be ordered in bulk at a discounted price (UK only).

Scripture quotations from the World English Bible.

Cover photograph by Rakicevic Nenad.

To the Reader –

This little booklet seeks to open up to the enquirer the truth about the nature of God's love: His love in action in His created world, and His love for people in particular.

For those who know the Lord and have experienced His wonderful love personally, the author seeks to underscore His utter trustworthiness and boundless patience with us, His children. God's faithful dealings with His people throughout the ages - recorded for us in His Word, the Bible - help us to grow in understanding and confidence as we walk with Him as His disciples in this world.

For those readers who do not yet know the Lord, the author prays that the words of this book would speak powerfully and persuasively, birthing the hope that you also may find your place in the family of God. May these thoughts and words speak to the deepest needs of each heart.

An unshakeable conviction of God's great love for us from before time itself, revealed to us in the works of Jesus Christ, is the surest foundation a life in this world may be built upon. Biblical truths about divine love, although presented here ever so briefly, should they be permitted to do so, will change the reader's view of God and His created world, and transform both their earthly and their eternal prospects.

God bless,

Carol Sullivan Johnson, Halstead, UK.

Contents

1. *God, the Originator of Love*

In our modern era, there is a tendency to associate love only with emotion. Movies, songs and novels often revolve around the quest for emotional fulfilment through romantic encounters. It may seem to us that finding that one, special, 'right' person will fulfil every emotional need. Our definition and expectation of love can be very narrow, rather romantic, and our quest for it quite elusive. We may extend our feelings of love to our families – parents, children, brothers and sisters, close friends, or even our pets. Some people express love for their possessions, their careers, or their hobbies.

Human love, charged as it may be with great emotion, is but the faintest echo of the highest and most powerful love through which the universe continues to be upheld. Human love is a poor imitation of the love that was first moved to form the worlds and all that they contain.

God's divine love is the origin of all love.

Sadly, many people in this world live life with little or no experience of love – either human or divine.

The Bible, which explains to us who we are and how we came into being, tells us firstly that God, by His own nature, defines love, and secondly, that He made people to be in His image.

Beloved, let's love one another, for love is of God … for God is love. (1 John 4:7-8)

And also:

God said, *"Let's make man in our image, after our likeness." (Genesis 1:26)*

God's purpose in making us in His image was so He could love us as a Father. We would be human sons and daughters of our Father God, and companions to His Son. He wanted to have fellowship with us, enjoy our company and share the wonderful world He had provided for us as a home. He intended humanity to have authority over our world as His representatives, in the same way He has authority over all His creation.

The Bible assures us that God was pleased with all that He had made in creation, including the first man and woman. They brought Him great pleasure.

God saw everything that he had made, and, behold, it was very good. (Genesis 1:37)

The Lord demonstrated His pleasure at the company of the man and woman He had created by walking and talking with them in the cool of the evening in their perfect garden home.

The story of creation and how sin came into our world (and the subsequent curse which came upon it through the disobedience of God's first human children) can be found in the very first chapters of the first book of the Bible – the *Book of Genesis*.

Love is not just an emotion – love is a motivating force.

The created universe shows us the enormity of the power that works through God, who defines Himself as 'love', and is motivated by that love. Divine love is sufficiently powerful to have created all that exists from nothing, and to continue to uphold it and all it contains, every moment of every day.

His Son (through whom the worlds were created) is the radiance of his glory, the very image of his substance, and upholding all things by the word of his power... (Hebrews 1:3)

Divine love, after which human love was modelled, is far above and beyond our natural human experience and understanding. God's divine nature expresses the purest, the highest, the most powerful, the original, authentic and everlasting force which we can comprehend love to be. Love is an aspect of God's eternal and unchanging character and personality.

God's love could not be shared with people unless He first created us with the capacity to give and receive love ourselves. So God made the first two people to be able to love – firstly to love Him, as their Maker and their God, and secondly, to love others. They were intended to fill the earth with offspring who also could live in the light of God's holiness, enjoying and reciprocating His love.

Our natural capacity to love God as He loves us was lost when the relationship He enjoyed with the first of His human children, Adam and Eve, was destroyed. Their disobedience brought upon them such great shame that they hid them Him, and all their offspring since have been born in the same state.

We are children of disobedience from birth, and as we grow, we quickly learn to follow our natural, base instincts. The inner workings of our sinful nature drives the passions of our bodies and we spend much of our lives taming them. We can no longer openly see or hear God, let alone love Him.

Having lost the glory of our original perfection and our access to the presence of God, all people have been left with is human love. Human love may shine like a star in the night sky, but the great glory of the love of God swallows up our little twinkling night star like the blazing light of the noonday sun. God's glorious love, like the fiercest midday sun, is too intense for us even to gaze upon.

The Bible recounts occasions when the Lord has afforded a glimpse of His glory to ordinary men – to the prophets who spoke for Him – but they were not able to endure it. They could not bear to stand before God. The light of God's holy presence showed up the filthiness of their own beings. Here are a few examples:

Isaiah, God's great prophet, saw a vision of the Lord seated upon His throne and cried, *"Woe is me, for I am ruined. I am a man of unclean lips…" (Isaiah 6:5)*

The prophet Ezekiel fell on his face at the vision of God's heavenly glory, and had to be raised up to his feet by God's Spirit.

This was the appearance of the likeness of Yahweh's (the Lord's) glory. When I saw it, I fell on my face, and I heard a voice of one that spoke. He said to me, "Son of man, stand on your feet, and I will speak with you." The Spirit entered into me when he spoke to me, and set me on my feet; and I heard him who spoke to me. (Ezekiel 1:28 and 2:1-2)

Moses, God's most faithful servant, was only able to look at His back after He had passed by.

Moses said, "Please show me your glory."

He said, "I will make all my goodness pass before you, and will proclaim Yahweh's (the Lord's) name before you...You cannot see my face, for man may not see me and live." (Exodus 33:18, 20)

The revelation of our wrong thoughts and actions, even the most secret of them, would cover us with unbearable shame if exposed by the light of God's holiness. Should He approach us, we would flee from Him. We can no longer fellowship with Him face-to-face, and even worse than that, the Bible says we have made ourselves His enemies and we hate Him. It is our sin – our own wrong-doing – which has caused this great rift between ourselves and our Maker.

But your iniquities have separated you and your God, and your sins have hidden his face from you, so that he will not hear. (Isaiah 59:2)

And so there is a great, impassable gulf of our own making fixed between us and God, our loving heavenly Father. We cannot receive God's pure love for us, and we cannot offer our tainted and inferior love to Him, even if we wanted to.

To overcome this dilemma and be restored to fellowship, or 'be reconciled' to God, a way for us to cross over to Him, and for Him to cross over to us, had to be established. Jesus, who was both God and human, is that Way. He is God's only Son, who truly understands humans because He became one, and the only human who truly understands God because He is God.

Jesus came down to live amongst us so He could teach us and show us what God the Father is really like.

2. God's Love in History

God's love is not sentimental. It is strong – fearsome even – and has been a motivating force behind His interventions in human affairs down through the ages.

Psalm 136 celebrates God's faithful love repeatedly:

Oh, give thanks to the God of heaven, for his loving-kindness endures forever.

The Bible speaks much about God's love. His great love for His creation and the people who inhabit our world is expressed throughout His Word. Here are two examples:

But you, Lord, are a merciful and gracious God, slow to anger, and abundant in loving kindness and truth. (Psalm 86:15)

And also:

But God commends his own love toward us, in that while we were yet sinners, Christ died for us. (Romans 5:8)

Sometimes we misunderstand God's love when we read stories from the Bible that are violent and gruesome. We ask, "How could a loving God do those things?" But we must not lose sight of the fact that God acted always to protect His beloved people against the rampant evil of their immoral idol-worshipping neighbours. In deepest spiritual darkness, they sacrificed their own babies to their false gods, offering them alive on fiery altars. Their evil practices would be as abhorrent to us today as they were to the Lord, and so should they be. If anyone behaved in such a way today, we would all be crying out for justice.

...every abomination to Yahweh (the Lord), which he hates, they have done to their gods; for they even burn their sons and their daughters in the fire to their gods. (Deuteronomy 12:31)

10

We can be assured that the judgement of God that fell on nations of the past was an entirely just and proportionate reaction to their own evil deeds. It was because of the wickedness of humanity that God chose out for Himself one family through whom He kept alive His knowledge on the earth. They were the children of Abraham through his grandson, Israel.

Because He made people to be able to exert free will, God allows the leaders of nations to pursue their aims. In their struggle for power and dominance, nation rises against nation and, as is always the case, the innocent bystanders are not spared. It is people who declare war on other people. We see this in our world today. God does not rain down bombs on women and children – other people do. Thankfully the Lord does intervene to limit their power and frustrate their ambitions!

Where do wars and fightings among you come from? Don't they come from your pleasures that war in your members? You lust, and don't have. You murder and covet, and can't obtain. You fight and make war. (James 4:1-2)

Rather than hating people, the Lord God of Israel actually welcomed any foreign person who wanted to be a part of His family on earth. His law made provision for them – offering refuge and protection should foreigners seek it amongst His people. He healed the sick foreigners who sought Him out, as in the case of Naaman, the great Syrian general, whose story can be found in *2 Kings 5*. In fact, the Lord even elevated two foreign women (who should have had no place in the nation of Israel at all) into Jesus's own direct family line!

One of these ladies was called 'Ruth' and her story is to be found in the *Book of Ruth*, in the Old Testament. She was a Moabitess – people outside the family of Israel – but her desire to be part of God's people led her ultimately to a position of great honour as the grandmother of Israel's King David.

Another stranger, named Rahab, an inhabitant of Jericho and an immoral woman, asked for mercy and pardon for herself and her family when her home city of Jericho was about to be attacked and overcome. Her story can be found in the Old Testament, in the ***Book of Joshua, chapter 2.***

When we understand the extent of evil and corruption that covered the earth, and God's willingness to pardon those who repented of their evil, we can see that God's mercy is freely available to all the people of the earth. Even whole cities of pagan idolaters could find themselves recipients of God's mercy.

Many of us may know the story of the prophet Jonah, who spent three days and nights in the belly of a huge fish. What we may not realise is the main point of the story.

Jonah had been told to go and warn the inhabitants of Nineveh, the capital of the feared Assyrian Empire, to turn away from their evil ways or the Lord's judgement would surely fall upon them. Nineveh was a huge city full of idol worshippers and greatly feared. We know from secular history that their army was mercilessly cruel, beyond imagination, to their defeated enemies. Jonah (and probably everyone else, too) did not care for the inhabitants of Nineveh. Why should they receive mercy?

The full story of how God set out to call a heathen people to repent, and His willingness to forgive wickedness where there is genuine repentance, can be found in the Old Testament in the ***Book of Jonah.***

Another story from the Bible – the story of Lot, Abraham's nephew – shows us how willing God is to pardon where He sees the slightest hope of salvation. From a whole town sunk in immorality, violence, and corruption, the Lord delivered one righteous man, Lot, and his family. Had He found just ten righteous souls in the community, for the sake of those ten, the whole town would have been spared. The story can be found in the Old Testament, in ***Genesis, chapters 18 and 19.***

The Lord takes no pleasure in suffering, death and destruction. He never rejected anyone who came to Him with a contrite heart, seeking forgiveness and acceptance as one of His own. He never turned anyone away who came to Him in faith…or even hope!

"Say to them, 'As surely as I live, declares the Sovereign LORD, I take no pleasure in the death of the wicked, but rather that they turn from their ways and live. (Ezekiel 33:11)

At times, the Lord was provoked to anger with the behaviour of His own chosen people, but He quickly remembered His love for them and the promises He had made to them. Like a father, the Lord scolds, corrects and chastises, but His love never fails. Like a husband, He loves and protects His people and yearns for their reciprocated faithfulness.

For your Maker is your husband, the LORD of hosts is his name; and the Holy One of Israel is your Redeemer, the God of the whole earth he is called. (Isaiah 54:5)

In the stories of the Old Testament, before He opened up a new and better way for us (which is what being a Christian is all about) the Lord pleaded with His people through His prophets to remain faithful in their worship, as they had promised that they would. He called out to them repeatedly to turn their backs on the evil religious practices and the false idols of their pagan neighbours.

An example of how God Himself tried to reason with His people and show them the folly of idol worship can be found in *Isaiah 44:16-17.* He is speaking about wood.

He burns half of it in the fire, and he roasts meat on that half.
He eats the roast and is satisfied.
Indeed, he warms himself and says, "Ah! I am warm; I see the fire."
From the rest he makes a god, his graven image.
He bows down to it and worships;
he prays to it and says, "Save me, for you are my god."

The Lord called to His people to honour the vows of faithfulness and obedience they had made to Him, like those exchanged between a husband and wife. Every time they turned their hearts back to Him, He forgave them and received them with great joy, promising even greater blessings and rejoicing.

God's love has never changed. From the days in which the worlds came into being and He made humanity in His image, His love for His creation has never waned.

We are the ones who have lost sight of Him. Our spirits within us are dead to Him. We cannot see, hear or know Him until He births within us a new, spiritual life. Our human reasoning, originally designed to be able to commune with the creator of the universe, is now debased by our own sinfulness. Our determination to live independently of Him, serving our own interests and desires, leads us into a life of bondage and shame. We stubbornly deny our spiritual need.

And yet God our Father still yearns for us to know Him and be restored to His eternal human family. Even today, when one living soul sees their spiritual state, their need to be forgiven, and returns to the loving arms of our heavenly Father, all the mightiest, majestic, gloriously holy angels in heaven rejoice.

"Even so, I (Jesus) tell you, there is joy in the presence of the angels of God over one sinner repenting." (Luke 15:10)

3.   The Unique Privilege of Humanity

The Bible tells us that the heavenly angels do not understand why God chose to redeem the fallen and corrupt, sinful human race.

For most certainly, he doesn't give help to angels, but he gives help to the offspring of Abraham. (Hebrews 2:16)

Angels did not have the privilege of a second chance extended to them when they rebelled against God, despite their infinitely superior heavenly power and beauty.

Have you ever wondered why God would redeem people, with our funny faces, our crooked teeth, our wrinkles and our bad habits, when He did not redeem Lucifer, the most magnificent and gifted angel who had stood by His very throne?

When Lucifer allowed himself to be lifted up by his own pride and ambition to challenge God for His throne, he and his subservient cohorts were all cast out of heaven. Some light is shed upon the events of Lucifer's fall in *Isaiah 14, Ezekiel 28* and in *Revelation 12:9*. He is no longer known as 'Bringer of Light' or 'Morning Star', but 'satan', 'the devil' or 'the evil one'.

There is no redemption for Lucifer and His fallen angels, but neither do they feel any remorse for their actions. They continue to kill, hate and destroy, because (said Jesus) it is in their nature to hate God and all that is His.

Those people on the earth who kill, hate and destroy are following in their father's footsteps, being children of wrath, just as their father, the devil, before them.

You are of your father the devil, and you want to do the desires of your father. He was a murderer from the beginning and doesn't stand in the truth, because there is no truth in him. When he speaks a lie, he speaks on his own; for he is a liar and the father of lies. (John 8:44)

15

There are only two types of people in this world – those who live under the dominion of the ruler of this world, which is his dark kingdom (the natural life into which we are all born) and those who have been translated out of that kingdom and into the kingdom of light (the kingdom of the Son of God being built upon the earth).

Those who would turn away from the kingdom of this world and enter God's spiritual kingdom on earth must be born into it via a second birth: a spiritual birth. This new birth comes only through faith in the saving intervention of Jesus Christ. Understanding and accepting Jesus's saving works gives entrance into a new type of life: spiritual life. There is no halfway house, nor alternative spiritual paths to God.

Both types of individuals exist, side by side, in every nation on earth. The natural person, be they overtly good or bad in their outward demeanour, lives in ignorance of the life-giving force of God's love for them. The person who has met God and accepted Him as their Lord and Saviour lives a life that has another dimension. They are alive to God through the power of His own eternal life which has come to reside within.

In the devil's world system, there are two extremes of people. Some learn to control their wrongful urges and live lawful, disciplined lives, doing good works outwardly, but knowing the principles of sin still working inside them. Other people give themselves over completely to their sinful urges, acting out their violent and hateful, destructive impulses, being slaves to their addictions, destroying themselves and others. And there is every category of person in between.

Whether outwardly good or manifestly evil, all are trapped in their own corrupt inner nature and ultimately, captives of the evil one. The Bible explains:

Since then the children have shared in flesh and blood, he (Jesus) also himself in the same way partook of the same, that through death he might bring to nothing him who had the power of death, that is, the devil, and might deliver all of them who through fear of death were all their lifetime subject to bondage. (Hebrews 2:14-15)

Sometimes the most unlikely people become Christians, because faith in Jesus is not dependent on how 'good' (or even how 'bad') somebody may have been. We cannot deserve God's mercy by impressing Him with our best efforts to be holy and good. And no one is so bad that they cannot be forgiven, should they repent and turn to the Lord to be made clean and whole.

The point about the mercy and grace of God in reaching down to us is that it is God's choice to love us and save us, not because of some innate 'goodness' or any efforts we make to appease Him.

The word 'grace' means 'undeserved favour'. God's choice to be merciful to us and freely pardon our sins is a matter between the Father and His Son. Before the world even existed, it was agreed between themselves that Jesus would offer Himself to His Father as our substitute to receive humanity's just reward – death.

When Jesus came to our world, He did more than teach us about God. At the end of His life, He diverted all God's judgement and righteous anger at our sin into His own body. He was brutally beaten and tortured, then nailed to a Roman cross where He ultimately surrendered His life. It was there that the Father's righteous judgement on humanity's sin was pronounced and the full force of His holy indignation and wrath against sin was poured out upon His Son, Jesus. Jesus took all our sin upon Himself and He paid for it utterly by sacrificing His life.

We can only ask that we may be included in God's family because of what Jesus did, not because of anything we have done, or promise to do. We cannot undo our offences. We cannot earn God's favour. Jesus earned God's favour for us, on our behalf, by being a perfect human Son, just as He is a perfect divine Son. Our Father extends His favour to include us as well when we accept Jesus, believing what He has done on our behalf and receiving Him into our lives. His perfect humanity becomes our perfect humanity, as far as the Father is concerned.

God's love still motivates Him to call His lost children home. His divine love has opened up the way for them to come.

Jesus is our second chance. The Bible says He is our second Adam – the one human who obeyed God instead of the first ones who disobeyed Him. He stood in the place of judgement for Adam and his descendants – the multitude of people who, like their father Adam, continue to disobey God. Those who put their trust in Jesus will never face God's righteous anger for their sin. They will stand before God's judgement throne and point to Jesus's wounds – the evidence that the penalty for their wickedness has been paid in full.

We can change the course of our lives by coming to the cross of Jesus Christ, laying down all that we are, and accepting the pardon and forgiveness He offers there. We can 'put on' the new life He offers: an endless, eternal life, at peace with God. Rather than remaining enslaved to the world and to our own passions, we can accept God's free pardon and the gift of new life, united with our Saviour, Jesus, through His Holy Spirit, which He gives to us. We can stand before God, accepted, clean, blameless and holy, clothed no longer in our own disobedience and sinful deeds, but in the obedience and righteousness of Jesus.

Or, we can reject the Lord's gracious offer, continue to live our own lives on our own terms and face the judgment throne of God hoping that our own personal good works will stand up to the scrutiny of the great Judge (and all our wicked deeds remain hidden from His glorious, unapproachable light). This would be the height of folly.

The Bible warns us already that *"there is no one righteous, no, not one." (Romans 3:10)*, so we may be certain in advance that we will not be judged as those who have done right through our own merits. God's judgement will surely fall against those who reject His only given means of finding forgiveness and pardon for crimes against Himself and against others.

There is salvation in no one else, for there is no other name under heaven that is given among men, by which we must be saved! (Acts 4:12)

If we comprehend the great privilege afforded to people above that of the angels, for whom there is no second chance, and refuse it, surely we must stand in greater condemnation than they. Rejecting God's loving and kind invitation to become one of His saved children will be our own eternal undoing.

4. Holiness and Justice meet Love and Mercy

Sometimes we hear people reason, "Well, if God was a God of love, why does He let terrible things happen? Why doesn't He just forgive everyone and accept them all into His presence? If He forgives some, why not all? Isn't that unfair?"

God is utterly just. He sets the standard on holiness, truth and justice.

The Apostle Paul explains to us: *"The wages of sin is death." (Romans 6:23)* All our wickedness, disobedience, stubborn rebellion and deceitfulness brings only death and destruction. It will earn us only the sentence of conscious, eternal separation from God.

In forgiving our sin, God has not simply chosen not to notice it. God's holiness demands that sin be judged and the life of the sinner forfeited.

The first and foremost characteristic of God is holiness.

In the Bible, the Apostle Peter explains: *"...just as he who called you is holy, you yourselves also be holy in all of your behaviour, because it is written, "You shall be holy, for I am holy." (1 Peter 1:15-16)*

The only reason God is able to overlook our sin is because someone else has already been judged guilty and taken the punishment for it.

According to the nature of our humanity, we cannot be acceptable to a holy God. Try as we may, we just cannot live a perfect, sinless life. Even if we strive to be good most of the time, we are still accountable for those times when we are not.

From the youngest age, we rage when our wills are crossed, steal other people's belongings, refuse to obey the simplest requests, and lie when we are caught doing something we know we shouldn't. We lash out in temper at those who love us most. And that's just by the age of two!

As we grow and become accountable for our contraventions of God's law, which our consciences alert us to, our wilful ways and misdeeds become a stain upon our inner persons. Although they may not always be visible to other people, they are certainly visible in the light of God's holiness. We are destroyed inside by giving in to our own wrong desires. We are the exact opposite of loving and obedient spiritual children.

But each one is tempted when he is drawn away by his own lust and enticed. Then the lust, when it has conceived, bears sin. The sin, when it is full-grown, brings forth death. (James 1:14-15)

Even those of us who spend their lives pursuing holiness in order to reach God die in our quest unsuccessful. The pursuit of personal holiness never ends, and can never be achieved through the discipline of our own will. To believe we can achieve the holiness of God through good works, mental discipline or altered consciousness is to be seriously ignorant of God's exalted glory and majesty. We cannot attain it, and we cannot contain it in our human experience.

God's holiness and His righteousness exist in perfect balance with His mercy and His love. God's perfect holiness (which demands holiness in those who dwell in His presence) and God's justice (which never deviates from the truth) must be accommodated alongside His love for His creation and His desire to be merciful – all being essential attributes of God's nature. All must be equally satisfied.

The Bible testifies:

The Rock (Jesus): his work is perfect, for all his ways are just. A God of faithfulness who does no wrong, just and right is he. (Deuteronomy 32:3-4)

And also:

All of your words are truth. Every one of your righteous ordinances endures forever. (Psalm 119:160)

According to the great love of God for His creation, He was not willing that all His human children should be eternally lost. A solution to this conundrum was needed. Someone had to pay the debt owed to a righteous God by His sinful people. Someone had to make up the shortfall. It was achieved at the cross of Jesus Christ.

The cross of Jesus Christ is the only place on earth where God's holy demand for justice was fully equalled and satisfied by an act of His own immense mercy and love.

We cannot undo our guilty actions, so we cannot save ourselves. Even if we could be perfect from this day onwards, we would still be guilty and liable for the debts of our past. Some people try to make up for their failings by doing extra good work. They may spend their whole lives striving to attain 'holiness'.

This is a terrible mistake to make. It demonstrates a lack of understanding about how God keeps his accounts of our actions, or lack thereof. In God's economy, holiness and perfection are demanded at all times. This is what is expected of the holy creatures that serve God in heaven.

If we were to look at it from an accounting point of view, God's balance sheet may look something like this:

On an account ledger, God's orders for holiness put us into a negative balance (we owe Him obedience) and we must fulfil those commands to discharge the debt, bringing our account back to zero – nothing owed. When we fail to obey God's holy commands, we chalk up for ourselves more and more 'debits' until we cannot even keep track of what we owe.

Because perfect obedience in all things is only what is expected, there is no opportunity to put aside extra 'credits' to cancel out our debt. Only someone who always obeyed God and never moved away from that place of perfect balance could ever hope to stand before God and not be found wanting. Jesus is the only human being to ever accomplish this.

Good works cannot cancel out bad. Good works only fulfil the debt their doer owes to God in the first place. Unless our bad works are cancelled for us, we cannot compensate for them in any way.

Only God could provide a solution to our dilemma, and His solution was as breath-taking in its profoundness as it was in its simplicity. His plan was to discharge the full penalty for our sin onto one human being, who represented all His children on earth, and let the children go free. He would lay the sins of His human sons upon His divine Son, who became human, like us, in order to represent us fully.

Jesus simply swapped places with us.

And so God gave us His innocent Son, Jesus, born into a human body as one of us, to take our guilt as if it was His own, to take the penalty for our wicked actions and thoughts as if He had committed them Himself. God poured out all His anger at the wrong-doing of His human family in all places, at all times, onto the human body of His Son.

Jesus was crucified with both the weight of our sins, and the wrath of His Father upon Him, and when He died, the penalty for all our sins was fully paid up. They were discharged and put aside forever.

The Father's anger at our wickedness was totally spent and His demand for the just punishment of our wrong-doing was completely satisfied. Our sin died there, on the cross, in the body of the only perfect human - Jesus Christ.

Jesus died instead of us. He paid the wages of all our guilty sins, past, present and future. The greatest demonstration of love, said Jesus, *"...was that a man lay down his life for his friends." (John 15:13)*

At the cross, the Son of God laid down His life for us so we could be pardoned, but His great plan of salvation did not end with pardoning our guilt for sin. Not only did Jesus, in His humanity, surrender His perfect life as a substitute for our wicked lives, but His Father accepted His perfect human life (that He lived on the earth, always pleasing His Father and obeying Him in all things) as if it were ours!

Jesus took our sin and shame upon Himself and died because of it. He offers us, in its place, His righteousness before His Father. Being God's Son, He had enjoyed untainted fellowship and love with His Father from before time began. Then, born into a human body, living on the earth, He continued to do only the things that pleased His Father. He was, and always will be, the only truly holy human being to ever live in His own right.

The transaction is illustrated in the Bible metaphorically as the wearing of clothes. Our best efforts are like wearing a filthy rag before God, so He took it from our shoulders and put it upon Jesus as if it were His. Jesus's pure, white robe of true goodness was taken from Him in exchange and laid upon us, as if it had always been ours – as if we had done those things.

For we have all become like one who is unclean, and all our righteousness is like a polluted garment. (Isaiah 64:6)

And also:

I will greatly rejoice in the Lord! My soul will be joyful in my God, for he has clothed me with the garments of salvation. He has covered me with the robe of righteousness. (Isaiah 61:10)

We contributed nothing to this transaction - except our sin. Nothing is required of us except that we believe in Jesus Christ and accept His gracious offer. We may come back into God's presence, restored and forgiven, knowing Him and knowing His love for us, simply by asking. The Holy Spirit will do what is necessary within us to bring it about.

But God, being rich in mercy, for his great love with which he loved us, even when we were dead through our trespasses, made us alive together with Christ ... that in the ages to come he might show the exceeding riches of his grace in kindness toward us in Christ Jesus; for by grace you have been saved through faith, and that not of yourselves; it is the gift of God ... (Ephesians 2:4-8)

5. *Demonstrating Divine Love*

What, exactly, does God's love look like in practical terms? Remember, God's love is a motivating force. It produces actions.

We have looked at how God's love prompted Him to create the first people so He could enjoy loving them as children. We have seen how, through disobedience, those people lost their innocence and their ability to come directly into His presence. We know that He sent His Son as a Saviour, to rescue them and us, their lost descendants.

Perhaps the clearest view we have of God's enduring love for people is that which we have of the life and actions of Jesus during His ministry on earth.

Jesus lived and walked alongside the ordinary folk of the day and did many miracles among them. He always maintained that it was only in obedience to the Father that He spoke and acted.

Jesus, therefore, answered them, "Most certainly, I tell you, the Son can do nothing of himself, but what he sees the Father doing. For whatever things he does, these the Son also does likewise." (John 5:19)

So what were the things that Jesus did in obedience to the Father? How did Jesus demonstrate to the people He lived amongst that God loved them?

Jesus claimed that His works among the people showed that He was sent by God.

In that hour he cured many of diseases and plagues and evil spirits, and to many who were blind, he gave sight. Jesus answered them, "Go and tell John the things which you have seen and heard: that the blind receive their sight, the lame walk, the lepers are cleansed, the deaf hear, the dead are raised

26

up, and the poor have good news preached to them." (Luke 7:21-22)

Jesus didn't just talk about God's love to the people who flocked to hear Him, He **showed them** God's love. He broke the chains of their oppression from sickness, poverty, social exclusion, mental torment, and all their associated conditions. He restored individuals to health and wholeness.

Jesus conveyed God's message of His enduring love in real and practical ways.

In the story of the raising of Lazarus from the dead, we have a beautiful illustration of the true humility and compassion of the man, Christ Jesus.

Jesus knew that Lazarus would not remain in the grave, but He delayed answering the urgent summons for help made by Lazarus's two sisters, Mary and Martha, so God's glory in the miracle of raising Lazarus would be seen by all in their community. The story is to be found in the *Gospel of John, chapter 11.*

In this account, we come across the shortest sentence and one of the most enigmatic statements recorded in the Bible:

Jesus wept. (John 11:35)

This one short statement opens to us a glimpse of the great humanity and humility of the man, Christ Jesus. Although He knew in advance that God would raise Lazarus from the dead, still he was touched by the rawness and anger of Mary and Martha's overwhelming grief at the loss of their beloved brother.

Mary, Martha and Lazarus were His friends and counted amongst His wider group of disciples. He had spent time with them, enjoying the hospitality of their home. They had heard His teaching and witnessed His miraculous and compassionate acts of healing. Now, when they needed Him so desperately to help them, He was nowhere to be found. Unbelievably, their brother died and they had buried him, four days before Jesus even arrived at their home! Their Master, the miracle worker who professed to love them, had seemingly forsaken them.

Mary expressed her frustration and bewilderment the moment Jesus arrived nearby, falling on her face before Him.

Therefore when Mary came to where Jesus was and saw him, she fell at his feet, saying to him, "Lord, if you would have been here, my brother wouldn't have died." (John 11:32)

Jesus did not reply. He could have distanced Himself from her anguish, remained a little aloof and in control of His emotions. He could have defended Himself against her thinly-veiled accusation of negligence – justified His delay as obedience to His Father – but He didn't. Jesus allowed her pain to become His pain. In His humanity, He allowed Himself to be moved by the grief of His friends and identified Himself with them in it, even though He already knew that His Father would raise Lazarus from the dead.

At this moment, in this snapshot of the ministry of Jesus, we see the calibre of the man who would stand between us and our God as a High Priest, interceding for us. We see the Son of Man touched with the feelings of our infirmities; He who stands in the breach made between ourselves and our heavenly Father by our own sinfulness.

We see our human representative in heaven who knows our weaknesses, our fears and our failures, who feels our inner turmoil and anguish of soul, and rather than chastising us when we come to Him, He receives us. He heals us. He restores us.

Having then a great high priest who has passed through the heavens, Jesus, the Son of God, let's hold tightly to our confession. For we don't have a high priest who can't be touched with the feeling of our infirmities, but one who has been in all points tempted like we are, yet without sin. Let's, therefore, draw near with boldness to the throne of grace, that

28

we may receive mercy and may find grace for help in time of need. (Hebrews 4:14-16)

Such is the nature of the love of God who reached down to us through His Son, Christ Jesus.

The Apostle Paul speaks of the nature of God's divine love in his first letter to the Corinthian church.

Love is patient and is kind. Love doesn't envy. Love doesn't brag, is not proud, doesn't behave itself inappropriately, doesn't seek its own way, is not provoked, takes no account of evil; doesn't rejoice in unrighteousness, but rejoices with the truth; bears all things, believes all things, hopes all things, and endures all things. Love never fails. (1 Corinthians 13:4-8)

We may try hard to be loving, and sometimes we may succeed, sometimes we may fail, but God's love for us is constant and unfailing. However, when our hearts have been filled with the love of God, through a supernatural work of His Spirit in us, we are able to love Him, and love people, the way we are loved by God.

6.   *God's Love Today*

Possibly the best known and most often used verse from the Bible about God's love may be *John 3:16:*

For God so loved the world that he gave his one and only Son, that whoever believes in him shall not perish but have eternal life.

Have you ever stopped to wonder when God made that decision – the decision to give His Son's life for the sake of the world?

Was it at some point during Jesus's lifetime? Was it when He was born, or during His ministry? Was it because the religious leaders of His day would not listen to Him, so God had to make a new plan?

"Jerusalem, Jerusalem, you who kills the prophets and stones those who are sent to her! How often I wanted to gather your children together, like a hen gathers her own brood under her wings, and you refused!" (Luke 13:34)

Was it earlier than Jesus's time, when He realised the Jews could not keep the Law He had given to them through Moses on Mt Sinai and He needed a new way for them to worship Him?

"This is the covenant I will make with the people of Israel after that time," declares the LORD.

"I will put my law in their minds and write it on their hearts. I will be their God, and they will be my people." (Jeremiah 31:33)

Was it even earlier, after the great Flood of Noah's day, which He sent to cleanse the earth from humanity's continual violence and evil?

The LORD saw how great the wickedness of the human race had become on the earth, and that every inclination of the thoughts of the human heart was only evil all the time. The LORD regretted that he had made human beings on the earth, and his heart was deeply troubled. (Genesis 8:5-6)

Was it earlier still, after Adam and Eve fell from their place of fellowship with Him because they had disobeyed Him and became too ashamed to face Him?

The Lord spoke to them of a deliverer who would crush Satan's head:

"And I will put enmity between you and the woman, and between your offspring and hers; he will crush your head, and you will strike his heel." (Genesis 3:15)

Was that when He decided to substitute the life of His Son for the lives of His human children?

There are clues in the Bible that indicate that the decision God made to give His Son as a ransom for our us and save us from eternal death was made before the worlds were even created.

In eternity, God the Father planned to send Jesus, and Jesus the Son agreed to be sent – to redeem His creation from under its curse.

...knowing that you were redeemed, not with corruptible things like silver or gold, from the useless way of life handed down from your fathers, but with precious blood, as of a lamb without blemish or spot, the blood of Christ, who was foreknown indeed before the foundation of the world, but was revealed in this last age for your sake. (1 Peter 1:18-20)

Jesus's life's work on earth had many aspects to it. He came to show us what God the Father was really like by teaching the truth about God's kingdom. He used practical demonstrations, such as feeding crowds of people and healing those who were sick, blind, deaf or crippled. He even restored dead children to their grieving parents. Many of the miracles He did and the lessons He taught can be read about in the four gospels: *Matthew, Mark, Luke and John.*

Jesus came to deal with the sin that separated us from our Father God. He also came to purchase Himself a Bride (the Church) whose love and companionship He will enjoy for eternity.

He died to render the power of Satan impotent, being the first and only person holy enough to defy the natural processes of death and burst out from the grave. Now, having returned to His Father in heaven, He waits until this message of love and restoration is delivered to all the peoples of the earth.

But when the fullness of time had come, God sent forth his Son, born of woman, born under the law, to redeem those who were under the law, so that we might receive adoption as sons. (Galatians 4:4-5)

And also:

...He made you alive together with him, having forgiven us all our trespasses, wiping out the handwriting in ordinances which were against us. He has taken it out of the way, nailing it to the cross. (Colossians 2:13-14)

The offer of a new life in God's family is open today to all who would receive Jesus and give themselves to Him. In due course, the Lord will wrap up time and the end of the age will come. The Lord knows the end from the beginning.

I am the Alpha and the Omega, the First and the Last, the Beginning and the End. (Revelation 22:13)

The God of the Bible is a Father God, who loves His children with a Father's love.

He is God the Son, who existed eternally with the Father and willingly became human so He could build a bridge between us and His Father. He is Jesus, the Saviour of the world.

He is the Holy Spirit of the Father and of the Son, who has been sent out into the world to move upon the hearts of men and women and call them home.

The Holy Spirit is given as a Teacher and a Comforter to those who would receive Jesus. He recreates within us spiritual eyes and ears and fills our hearts with God's love. He guides us and strengthens us from within as we journey through this life. He unites us with Jesus Christ as our living head.

Today, Jesus still invites anyone and everyone who would believe in His saving work to come and join Him. He offers a new sort of life – eternal life, safe in the love of God – to any who would lay down their burden of sin, guilt and condemnation at the cross, turning away from it, and accept His offer of pardon, restoration and everlasting friendship.

7.   Our Love to God

To those readers who already know the Lord, let us learn from the Apostle John who was known for the emphasis he placed on the love of God as the motivating force of faith.   Without showing other people God's love in our words and our actions, says, John, we make our profession of faith in the Lord Jesus Christ a lie.

But God's love has most certainly been perfected in whoever keeps his word. This is how we know that we are in him: he who says he remains in him ought himself also to walk just like he walked. (1 John 2:5-6)

James, leader of the early church in Jerusalem, seems to concur when he speaks in his epistle about faith that does not evidence itself in good works.

Pure religion and undefiled before our God and Father is this: to visit the fatherless and widows in their affliction, and to keep oneself unstained by the world. (James 1:37)

And also:

But do you want to know, O foolish man, that faith without works is dead? (James 2:20)

The Apostle Paul agrees that God's divine love is the greatest abiding evidence and motivating force in the life of a disciple, so much so, that it will keep us in this life and take us all the way into eternity.

Who shall separate us from the love of Christ? Shall tribulation, or distress, or persecution, or famine, or nakedness, or peril, or sword? Nay, in all these things we are more than conquerors through him that loved us. For I am persuaded, that neither death, nor life, nor angels, nor principalities, nor powers, nor things present, nor things to come, nor height, nor depth, nor any other creature, shall be able to separate us from the love of God, which is in Christ Jesus our Lord. (Romans 8:35-39)

So, what does knowing and living in God's love look like in practical, modern-day terms? Is it sufficient to say we love God but behave in ways that are contrary to the example of our great Teacher, Jesus?

Does the Holy Spirit, our Teacher in this world, tell us that we may believe in Jesus, but have a different world view, an alternative morality, or a different personal agenda than that demonstrated by Jesus's life and ministry on earth? Isn't our purpose as children of God in this world to continue the works Jesus did and glorify His Name on the earth? Are we not to be like Him?

The great news is that the Holy Spirit overflows our hearts with God's love when He comes to give us His new life. When we are saturated with God's love for us, we can live in the power of that love and express it back to God as well as outwards to others. We can have a loving heart like Jesus because His Spirit of love has come to live within us.

Being therefore justified by faith, we have peace with God through our Lord Jesus Christ God's love has been poured into our hearts through the Holy Spirit who was given to us. (Romans 5:1, 5)

Let's look once again at the example given to us in the perfect human – Jesus. He was the embodiment of God's love and the expression of God's love for humanity in particular.

Jesus's choices and His decisions in His life on this earth were based on the loving relationship He enjoyed with His Father. As we have seen, He obeyed His Father in all things and the Father was always pleased with Him.

"He who sent me is with me. The Father hasn't left me alone, for I always do the things that are pleasing to him." (John 8:29)

Jesus taught that to be one of His disciples, we must be those who follow His example. As a disciple of Christ, we must live out our new lives with conviction and deliberate purpose, just as He did. We should be continuing to do the things that we see that Jesus did (through the testimony of the Gospels in the Bible).

Jesus's disciples should see truth the way Jesus saw truth. We should respond to the challenges of life the way Jesus responded. We are called to be His ambassadors in this world, and as His representatives, we put aside our own wills, our own agendas and our own interests, and 'take up the cross', following Him, according to His teaching, and after His example.

Then Jesus said to his disciples, "If anyone desires to come after me, let him deny himself, take up his cross, and follow me. For whoever desires to save his life will lose it, and whoever will lose his life for my sake will find it." (Matthew 16:24-25)

Throughout His ministry, Jesus showed us the heart of His Father. His life was one of service. He was a man of great compassion, humility and faith in the goodness of His Father.

Jesus showed us the love the Father has for us by meeting the needs of those whose lives He touched, those who sought Him out, and even by seeking out individuals Himself. His words were gracious and truthful. His nature was open and generous. He was motivated by divine love. But He was also uncompromising towards hypocrites who offered God lip-service, but whose lives did not honour Him.

The Word became flesh and lived among us. We saw his glory, such glory as of the only born Son of the Father, full of grace and truth. From his fullness, we all received grace upon grace. (John 1:14, 16)

As Christians, we are born into a body of believers. Originally, there was only one Jesus, but now there are millions of His followers who represent Him and the Father to the people of the earth. Our mission is to tell others that they can be restored to

God's family, knowing Him as their Father, and walking with Jesus as friend with friend.

Faithfully and effectively delivering God's promise of forgiveness and new life in Christ is the greatest message of love we can express to another human being in this world.

8.   An Invitation to a Personal Encounter with a Loving and Merciful Saviour

Dear Reader,

This little book could never tell all the glorious attributes and works of the Lord Jesus Christ, God's Son, who came to this world as the Saviour of lost souls. Neither could it fully express the great joy and peace that fills the hearts of those who, by faith in Jesus's life and death, return to the welcoming arms of their loving heavenly Father. But it can guarantee that there is no one breathing God's air on this earth, at this moment, who has no need of His love, mercy and grace. Neither is there anyone who is either too important or too insignificant to receive them.

There is no sin too great or too small that God won't forgive – if we believe that Jesus has already suffered for it. There is no life so damaged that He cannot make it whole again and restore it to Himself. Jesus doesn't want you to just believe He existed. He wants to change your life from the inside out. He wants to come and make His home with you.

God is the most accepting Being in existence. He does not discriminate against individuals on any grounds whatsoever – age, gender, race, colour, sexual orientation, disability, social status, nationality, political affiliation, nor any other category of person we may choose to invent. He invites every one of us to utterly cast off our old life of torment and sin and receive a new life of holiness and friendship with Him. If we want to accept His offer, He will accept us and change us through the life and power of His Holy Spirit who works in our hearts to accomplish the transformation. The life He offers in exchange for our torment of mind and brokenness of heart is one of inner rest and peace in Him.

In your presence is fullness of joy. In your right hand, there are pleasures forevermore. (Psalm 16:11)

Jesus, through His Holy Spirit who is given to us, breaks the power of our old, wicked nature and gives us the ability to choose to live a life that honours and pleases Him. Even though we may not always manage to resist the many temptations we find ourselves encountering, His sacrificial death ensured forever that we may come to Him continually to find mercy, forgiveness and restoration. His commitment to His children is complete and unfailing. We never need to fear that He will 'give up' on us.

If the words of this book have awoken in you a sense of need to find your way into a real and personal relationship with a loving Father God and His Son, Jesus, and you would like to know and walk with Jesus as your Saviour and friend, simply open your heart and ask Him to rescue you – to save you.

Jesus hears all your prayers – every single one – and knows every one of your thoughts as well as your deeds.

There is nothing too hard for God. Before you were born, He had already opened a way for you to be saved from eternal destruction. It was always His desire to bring you joyfully into His Father's house. And you may come, simply by putting your trust in Him. This is His great wish – that people who are scarred and tormented by life in this world may find healing and wholeness in His Kingdom. His invitation is personal, and it is directed right at you. Jesus promised us all:

"I am the way, the truth, and the life." (John 14:6)

Don't be like those who receive the seed of God's Word and understand it but let the issues of life choke it out until it can be heard no more. Listen to the convicting voice within, which is the voice of the Holy Spirit drawing you towards a life-changing encounter with the Living God.

Seek the Lord with all your heart. He has promised that He will enable you to find Him. He made that promise while He was on earth, and it was recorded for us in the Bible:

"Ask, and it will be given you. Seek, and you will find. Knock, and it will be opened for you. For everyone who asks receives. He who seeks finds. To him who knocks it will be opened." (Matthew 7:7-8)

We can come to Jesus without fear. He is never disappointed or angry with us, and He will never reject anyone who comes with honesty about their true needs.

You cannot make yourself better or more worthy to come to God. He knows full well you cannot fix yourself or make yourself acceptable to Him, and He does not ask you to. Jesus only asks you to trust Him and believe that what He and the Father have promised to do, will be done in you, in reality, by the power of His Holy Spirit.

Jesus's suffering and death on the cross paid for the sin of everyone who would accept Him. If you believe Him, receive Him and walk with Him, you will never be called to account for the sins of your past, present, or future ones, either. If you ask Him to, He will take away your sin and give you His righteousness from the moment you truly believe, and He will make you holy before His Father continually. Jesus will give you a whole new life to live out in this world, based on faith and friendship with Him.

Through His Holy Spirit, Jesus will do whatever is necessary to bring you back into relationship with God – things you cannot do for yourself. Jesus said that saving those who come to Him and giving them new and abundant life was His whole purpose in coming into the world and suffering as He did. The words below were also spoken by Jesus Himself:

"I am the door. If anyone enters in by me, he will be saved, and will go in and go out and will find pasture. The thief (Satan) only comes to steal, kill, and destroy. I came that they may have life, and may have it abundantly." (John 10:9-10)

Continue always in prayer and let the Lord lead you. Put your life in His hands. Jesus promises that if you come to Him, He will receive you. He will cleanse you inside and heal you. He will come and abide with you always.

We commit you, whoever and wherever you are, into His tender care. We believe what Jesus Himself said about the children His Father gives to Him, which is written here for you:

"All those whom the Father gives me will come to me. He who comes to me I will in no way throw out. For I have come down from heaven, not to do my own will, but the will of him who sent me.

This is the will of my Father who sent me, that of all he has given to me I should lose nothing, but should raise him up at the last day.

This is the will of the one who sent me, that everyone who sees the Son and believes in him should have eternal life; and I will raise him up at the last day." (John 6:37-40)

Dear Reader, you are personally invited to become a part of God's great salvation mission and His heavenly family, right here, and right now.

Will you say 'Yes' to Him?

The Spirit and the bride say, "Come!" He who hears, let him say, "Come!" He who is thirsty, let him come. He who desires, let him take the water of life freely. (Revelation 22:17)

Other books by The Barn Church Fellowship

Other publications by The Barn Church Fellowship include:

'God's Plan, God's Power', a seven-part Bible study series for group study or personal development in understanding the foundations of the New Covenant and Christian faith and practice.

'The Beyond Time and Space Man', a book for young teens about Jesus, the Son of Man, and His mission to rescue Planet Earth and its inhabitants from destruction.

If you have been blessed by the message in this booklet, please pass it on to someone else and bless them, too.

This booklet may be ordered in bulk by emailing:

contact.the.barnchurch@gmail.com

(UK postal addresses only).

Printed in Great Britain
by Amazon

86883628R00031

VOLUME 3

JADE'S EROTIC ADVENTURES - BOOK 3